IT'S SCIENCE!

Forces around us

IT'S SCIENCE!

Forces around us

Sally Hewitt

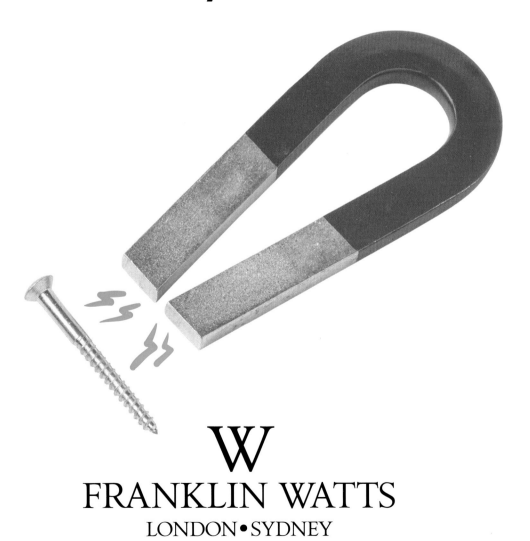

W

FRANKLIN WATTS
LONDON • SYDNEY

First published in 1997 by Franklin Watts
96 Leonard Street, London EC2A 4XD
Paperback edition 2000

Franklin Watts Australia
14 Mars Road
Lane Cove
NSW 2066

Series editor: Rachel Cooke
Art director: Robert Walster
Designer: Mo Choy
Picture research: Susan Mennell
Photography: Ray Moller unless otherwise acknowledged
Consultant: Sally Nankivell-Aston

A CIP catalogue record for this book
is available from the British Library.

ISBN 0 7496 2844 8 (hbk); 0 7496 3604 1 (pbk)

Dewey Classification 531

Printed in Malaysia

Photographic acknowledgements:
Robert Harding pp. 7bl (Gary Bingham), 11br (Rolf Richardson), 17l
Image Bank pp. 12b (Dimitris Talianis), 13tl (Bernard van Berg)
Images pp. 25l, 25r
Rex Features 26br
Telegraph Colour Library/Planet Earth pp. 25t (Georgette Douwma)
Tony Stone pp. 11bl (David Bjorn), 12l (Joel Rogers), 12c (Daniel Bassett), 21l (Vince Streano) 21r
Zefa pp. 13tr, 23l
The publishers would also like to thank NES Arnold Limited for the loan of the magnets that appear on
the cover, title page and pp. 10, 26, 27 and 29.
Thank you, too, to our models: Charlie Lucas, Georgina Walker, Jordan Morris-Hudson and Sumire Fujimoto.

Contents

Falling down

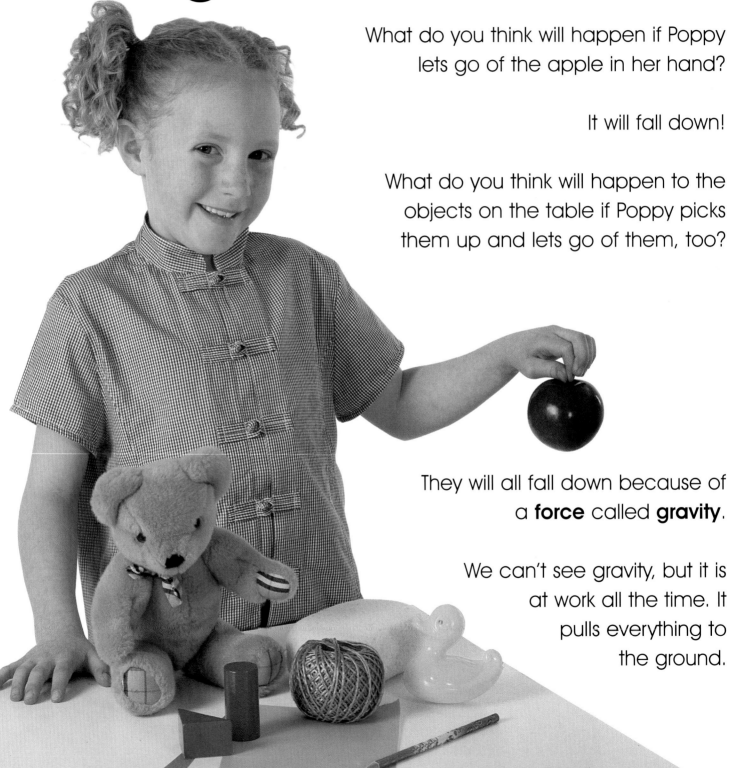

What do you think will happen if Poppy lets go of the apple in her hand?

It will fall down!

What do you think will happen to the objects on the table if Poppy picks them up and lets go of them, too?

They will all fall down because of a **force** called **gravity**.

We can't see gravity, but it is at work all the time. It pulls everything to the ground.

Air is all around us. We can't see air. But we feel it when we breathe in or when the **wind** blows.

Everything that drops has to fall through the air. Air can slow things down.

Air collects under a parachute as it falls and slows it down for a soft landing.

TRY IT OUT!

Find 2 pieces of paper exactly the same. Screw one piece into a ball. Drop them both and watch what happens.

Why do you think the flat paper floats down slowly and the screwed up paper falls straight down?

Heavy or light?

Do you know how much you weigh? **Scales** like those Charlie is standing on measure how **heavy** you are.

The scales tell Charlie that he weighs 25 kilograms.

Kitchen scales measure things that are much lighter than you, such as the ingredients for a cake.

It is gravity pulling down on an object that gives it **weight**.

Can you guess, just by looking at these objects, if they are heavy or **light**?

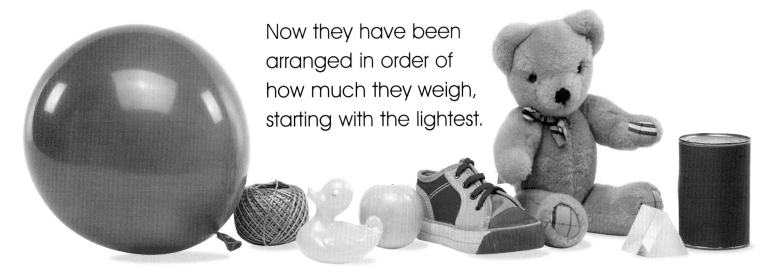

Now they have been arranged in order of how much they weigh, starting with the lightest.

⚡ TRY IT OUT!

Were you right?
Is the biggest object the heaviest?
Is the smallest object the lightest?

Collect some objects like these.
Guess which are the heaviest and the lightest.
Pick them up and feel gravity pulling on them.
Put them in order of weight – start with the lightest.

What is a force?

A force **pushes** or **pulls** an object and makes it move. The object may move faster or slower or change **direction**. A force can change the shape of an object, too.

Wind is a natural force that moves the pinwheel round and round as it blows.

The force of a **magnet** can pull metal objects towards it.

This ball is floating because the force of the water pushes the ball upwards.

 **TRY IT OUT!**

Push a light plastic ball like this down in some water. Feel the water pushing it up.

Force from your muscles can push and pull dough into different shapes.

Surfers ride on the force of the waves.

Force from this digger's powerful engine moves the pile of mud.

 **LOOK AGAIN**

Look again at page 6.
What force pulls the apple
to the ground?

Standing firm

How can a building stand firm even when gravity pulls it, the wind blows it or an earthquake shakes it?

Buildings are supported by foundations dug deep into the ground. Strong frames hold up the walls and floors.

Bricks are laid in patterns and stuck together with cement.

Some buildings are held up by columns.

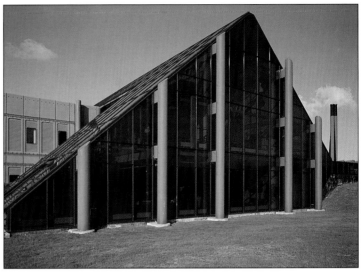

Buttresses prop up heavy walls.

Triangles are very strong. Look out for triangle shapes in all kinds of buildings.

 TRY IT OUT!

Have a competition with a friend to see who can build the strongest and tallest building.

Use wooden and plastic building bricks, cardboard tubes, sheets of cardboard, paper, straws and boxes. Think of ways to make your building strong. How will you test it?

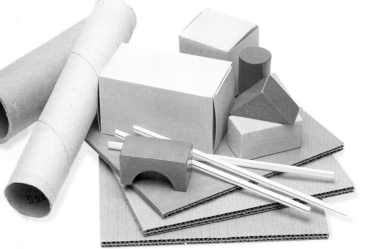

Push and pull

A toy car, a yogurt pot lid, a piece of paper and a zip cannot move or change by themselves.
A force can move or change them.

Someone has been busy!
Did they push or pull the car, the lid, the paper, and the zip to make them move and change?

14

Sometimes there are different forces pushing and pulling at the same time.

Charlie and Gemma are having a tug of war.
They are both pulling just as hard as each other.
No one is winning! They are staying in the same place.

What would happen if a friend joined in and helped
Gemma to pull? Would they still stay in the same place?
Why not?

 THINK ABOUT IT!

Charlie and Gemma's rope is strong so
it will not break when they pull it.
What would happen if they both pulled
as hard as they could on each end of
a cracker?

15

Press!

When you press a drawing pin into a pin-board, the force of your push goes onto the point.

The force of a hammer goes onto the point of a nail.

Needles have a sharp point, too.

Would it be easy to pin up a note, hammer a nail or sew if the thumb-tack, the nail and the needle were blunt?

You would have to push much harder!

TRY IT OUT!

Pull some paper tightly over an empty yogurt pot and fix it in place with an **elastic** band. Try to press the sharp end of a pencil through the paper. What happens? Try to push the blunt end through the paper. What happens now?

A tractor presses down heavily on soft mud, but it does not sink in. The weight of the tractor is spread over 6 wide tyres. There are no sharp points to sink easily into the mud!

THINK ABOUT IT!

What would happen if you tried to ride over mud on a bicycle with very thin tyres?

17

Squash and stretch

Pushes and pulls can **squash** and **stretch** things into different shapes.

When you pull elastic, like these braces, it stretches. When you let it go, the elastic snaps back again.

Elastic is very useful for keeping your trousers up! Can you see something else in the picture that elastic is useful for?

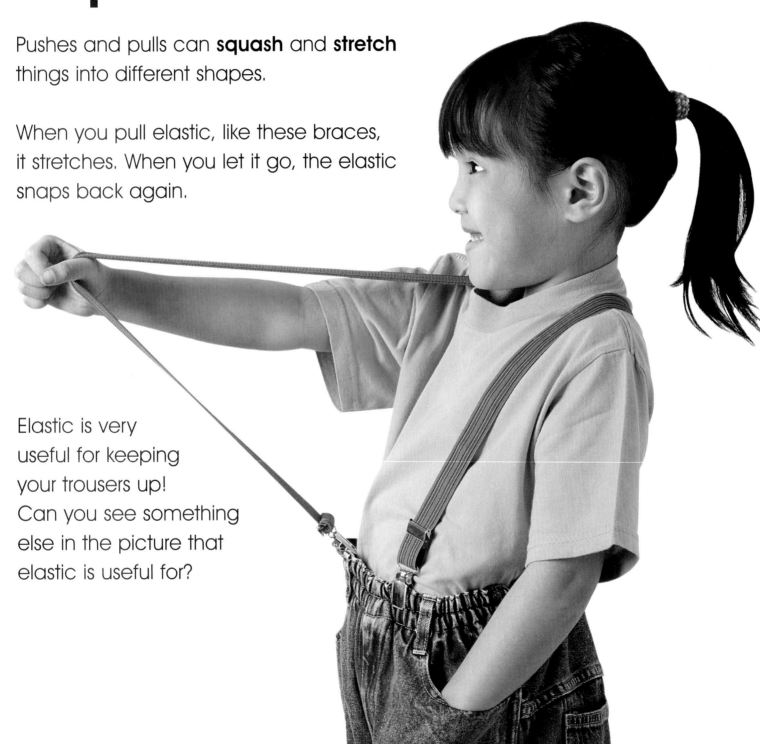

You can squeeze water out of a sponge. When you let the sponge go, it goes back into its usual shape.

When you squash and stretch modelling clay, it keeps the new shape you have given it.

TRY IT OUT!

Collect a plastic ruler, a pencil, paper, some poster putty, an elastic band and a sponge. Try squashing, stretching and bending them. (Don't stretch the elastic band so hard that it snaps.)

Notice all the different things that happen.

Start and stop

This toy truck will only move if it is pushed or pulled.

Poppy can push the truck to make it go.
She can pull the string at the back of the truck
to stop it. The harder Poppy pushes the truck,
the faster and the further it will go.

Joe can pull the string at the front
of the truck to make it go. He can
push the truck to make it stop.

TRY IT OUT!

Find a toy truck. How far can you make it go with one push?
Load the truck with bricks. What happens when you push or pull
the truck now? How can you make the truck slow down?
Try to make the truck change direction.

A gigantic oil tanker is very heavy. Once it gets going, it is very difficult to stop.

A heavy truck needs strong brakes to slow it down and stop it. The faster it goes, the harder it is to stop it quickly.

Bicycles are quite light, so they are easier to start and stop. You push on the pedals to move the bicycle along.

When you press the brakes, brake blocks push against the wheel rim to slow the bicycle down and stop it.

Rubbing together

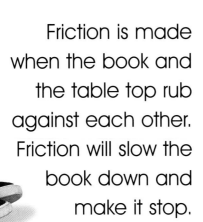

If you push a book across a table, it won't keep going for long.

It might bump into the pile of books or fall off the end of the table. It will probably slow down and stop before it reaches the books. This is because of a force called **friction**.

Friction is made when the book and the table top rub against each other. Friction will slow the book down and make it stop.

LOOK AGAIN

Look again at the bicycle on page 21. What happens when the brake blocks rub against the wheel? What force is at work?

Ice skates have to slip easily over ice. The blades are smooth and shiny so that there is as little friction as possible.

Friction can be useful. The sole of this shoe is rough and bumpy. It is specially designed to stop you slipping.

 TRY IT OUT!

Feel a table top, a carpet, grass or a stone path. Are they smooth or bumpy? Try pushing a box along on the different surfaces. What happens?

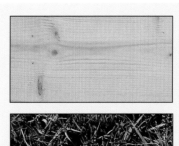

Drag!

Air slows down everything that tries to move through it.

An aeroplane and a racing car like these have **streamlined** shapes so that air can slip over them.

TRY IT OUT!

Move a piece of paper around you through the air. Can you feel the air pushing against it?

Fold the paper into a dart and throw it. Is the paper a better shape now for moving fast through the air?

Water slows down everything that tries to move through it, too.

Fish have streamlined bodies that move easily through water.

Look at the shapes of these boats. Which one do you think is the best shape for speeding along?

The force that slows things down in air and water is called **drag**.

👁 LOOK AGAIN

Look again at page 7. What is designed to fall slowly through the air?

Magnetism

Magnets like these pull objects made of iron or steel towards them.

They can do this because of a force called **magnetism**.

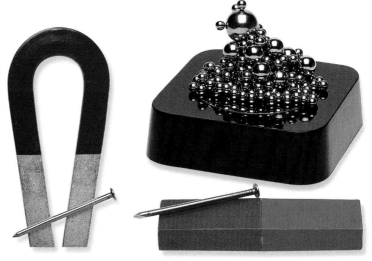

To buy:
milk,
eggs,
bread,
more fridge
magnets!

Some cranes use giant magnets to pick up metal.

TRY IT OUT!

Find a magnet. Collect some small metal objects like the ones in the picture.

Which ones will the magnet pick up? A magnet picks up the objects on the left from our collection.

Make a paper clip chain hanging down from your magnet.
How many paper clips are in your chain?

LOOK AGAIN

Magnetism is a force that you cannot see. Look back through the book. What other forces are at work even though you cannot see them?

Useful words

Air Air is a kind of gas. We can't see it but it is all around us. People, animals and plants all need air to live.

Direction When a thing moves from one place to another, it moves in a direction. It might go forwards, backwards, up, down, left or right.

Drag Drag is a type of force. Things moving through air and water are slowed down by drag.

Elastic Something elastic stretches when you pull it and springs back to its usual shape when you let it go.

Force A force pushes and pulls an object and makes it move, speed up, slow down, change direction or change shape.

Friction Friction is a type of force. It happens when two things rub against each other.

Gravity Gravity is a type of force. It pulls everything down to the ground.

Heavy Something is heavy if it weighs a lot. A big bag of shopping would feel heavy to pick up.

Light Something is light if it only weighs a little. An empty bag feels light to pick up.

Magnet A magnet pulls objects made of iron and steel towards it, using the force of magnetism.

Magnetism Magnetism is a type of force. It either pulls objects towards each other or pushes them apart.

Pull You can move an object or change its shape by pulling it. You pull things towards you.

Push You can move an object or change its shape by pushing it. You push things away from you.

Scales Scales are machines that measure how much things weigh.

Squash You squash an object when you push it to make its shape shorter or smaller. You can squash a sponge.

Streamlined Air and water slip easily over a streamlined shape. Racing cars, aeroplanes and speedboats have streamlined shapes for moving fast through air and water.

Stretch You stretch an object when you pull it to make its shape longer or wider. You can stretch elastic.

Triangle A triangle is a flat shape with three corners and three straight sides.

Weight Gravity pulling down on a object gives it weight. Weight is a type of force.

Wind Wind is made by moving air. It is a type of force.

Index

About this book

Children are natural scientists. They learn by touching and feeling, noticing, asking questions and trying things out for themselves. The books in the *It's Science!* series are designed for the way children learn. Familiar objects are used as starting points for further learning. *Forces around us* starts with a falling apple and explores forces.

Each double page spread introduces a new topic, such as magnetism. Information is given, questions asked and activities suggested that encourage children to make discoveries and develop new ideas for themselves.
Look out for these panels throughout the book:

TRY IT OUT! indicates a simple activity, using safe materials, that proves or explores a point.
THINK ABOUT IT! indicates a question inspired by the information on the page but which points the reader to areas not covered by the book.
LOOK AGAIN introduces a cross-referencing activity which links themes and facts through the book.

Encourage children not to take the familiar world for granted. Point things out, ask questions and enjoy making scientific discoveries together.